THIS
AMERICAN
MOMENT

***

THOUGHTS
ON THE
AMERICAN
CONDITION

*****

M.G. Montpelier

For information and/or comment address:
M.G. Montpelier, Epsom, NH 03234.

Consultant - Pauline Cusson
Cover Design by Jonnie Maloney
Photograph by Charlene Graham

ISBN: 978-1-4834-5443-6 (sc)
ISBN: 978-1-4834-5442-9 (e)

Library of Congress Control Number: 2016946120

Because of the dynamic nature of the Internet, any web addresses or links contained in this book may have changed since publication and may no longer be valid. The views expressed in this work are solely those of the author and do not necessarily reflect the views of the publisher, and the publisher hereby disclaims any responsibility for them.

Lulu Publishing Services rev. date: 7/11/2016

FOR

The People of America, es-
pecially, the poor, the downtrodden, the oppressed; the
homeless, the jobless, the hungry; the victims of duplicity,
deception, and deceit; and all
who suffer from the struggle,
violence, and injustice of this
American Moment.

"Something shattering has happened to our democracy. Something about the use of money and marketing in politics, the decline of both political parties ... something has caused the whole Washington establishment to lose its moorings to the people."[1]

-Donella Meadows
Who Will Tell the People?

CONTENTS

"Who Will Tell the People" [2]
-William Greider, 1992

"Money's conquest of American politics has... rendered impotent the well-worn prescriptions of the left and the right... Neither liberal nor conservative visions of good government can be realized as long as government itself is for sale." [3]

- Allison Stranger,
One Nation Under Contract

INTRODUCTION

"Democracy arises out of
the notion that those who
are equal in any respect are
equal in all respects."[4]
                                    - Aristotle

I have for many years studied with
great pride and joy the epic journey
of the American experience, from the
time of the Founding Fathers – those
pioneers of democracy and freedom,
Washington, Jefferson, and Madison, to
the defenders of liberty and representative government, Abraham Lincoln,
Theodore Roosevelt, and that champion
of the people, Franklin D. Roosevelt.

It was President Franklin D. Roosevelt
who brought a suffering people out
of the Great Depression and champi-

oned the Glass-Steagall Act of 1933, the cornerstone of the New Deal.

It was not so long ago when every American shared in some way the covenant of the "American Dream" – yesterday's promise of an America of opportunity for all working Americans, a prosperous middle class secure and stable, long-term productive employment, a progressive living wage, an affordable mortgage, medical care, and retirement, hopefully leaving their children better off than themselves.

It is with grave concern that I have followed America's industrial demise, the collapse of the "American Dream," the transfer of middle class prosperity to the megarich, and the making of a subsistence minimum-wage society incapable of employing its people and unable to provide the means for an average American family to sustain itself.

This American Moment endeavors to capture the frustration, the challenges, and uncertainty of a people suffering – a people struggling day-to-day to survive a predatory fairy-tale economic agenda legalized through cunning deregulation politics by a dysfunctional political system that brought about the "pooring of America."

May a renewal of the American Spirit, the soul of Freedom, Equality, and Justice that defines who we are as a people, triumph for all the people of America in this American moment.

M. G. Montpelier

"There is no nation on earth powerful enough to accomplish our overthrow. Our destruction, should it come at all, will be from another quarter. From the inattention of the people to the concerns of their government, from their carelessness and negligence. I must confess that I do apprehend some danger. I fear that... they may be made the dupes of designing men and become the instruments of their own undoing." [5]

-Daniel Webster

I

JUST COLLATERAL DAMAGE

*"The business of moving tradi-
tional jobs abroad – called
"outsourcing" has been one
of this country's few growth
industries… it means lower
wages and fatter profits. As
for the American workers
eliminated along the way,
they are just collateral damage."* [6]

- Bartlett & Steel,
*The Betrayal of the
American Dream*

**As the golden rays of
dawn peek through the
morning mist, I struggle
to rise from my**

slumber, my mind
   troubled, confused,
and restless.

Many friends yesterday
   lost their job to China
with the closing of the
   town's only source of
employment. I wonder
   with somber trepida-
tion, panic and alarm
   what is to become of us
- just another community
   bankrupt, desolate and
desperate in the heartland
   of America? - just
another American com-
   munity cast aside, its
people discarded and

abandoned as "just
collateral damage" in the
    rush for cheap labor
and big profits.

Staring in the stillness
    and warmth of morn-
ing's early light, I hesitate
    to presume who we are
as a people, a people nur-
    tured from birth we are
a people blessed to live in
    a democracy "of the
people,"[7] a free and dem-
    ocratic society "with
liberty and justice for
    all."[8]

I am distressed, saddened,
   and, confused for I
am mindful we are a
   people of "Liberty"
forged out of our ances-
   tors' struggle to be free
from outside influence
   and domination; a
people honest and
   hardworking, resilient
in adversity and eager for
   reform; a people of
resolve once awakened to
   right the inequities of
political and economic
   injustice.

I see the frustration, mis-
   fortune, and uncer-

4

tainty of this American moment need not be the future of the people of America. "We the People," citizens of this great democracy "of the people[9] do have "the right, the power, and the duty to protect (our) own welfare."[10]

II

YESTERDAY'S PROMISE

"The promise of the American Dream requires that we are all provided an equal opportunity." [11]

-Charles R. Rangel

Look closer, you'll find
I'm one like you who
seeks only to live in peace
and quiet, make ends
meet, and make it grace-
fully through another
day.

I'm that politically weary
American who longs to

believe in the "American
    Dream" – yesterday's
promise of opportunity
    and success for our
children and grandchil-
    dren.

I'm that American who
    cannot help but recall
those days not so long ago
    when America was at
economic peace, and we all
    took pride in a strong
middle class - prosperous,
    secure, and stable.

It was a time when
    America was a powerful
industrial giant, and

everyone had access to a
productive family-wage
    job, affordable medical
care, and the promise of a
    retirement with dignity
in old age.

It was the golden age of
    American democracy
when every youth's
    dreams were within
reach given hard work
    and perseverance, the
American moment we
    trusted in the assurance
the economic security of
    American capitalism
was the cornerstone of

America's freedom and democracy.

It was the grand moment of the American experience, a time we celebrated together in the belief of "one Nation under God,"[12] the sanctity of Freedom, Equality, and Justice, and acknowledged every person was endowed with the inalienable rights of "Life, Liberty and the pursuit of Happiness."[13]

The "affluent society" and all that made America

the economic miracle of
    the world is gone now –
dismantled and discarded
    in the name of fairy-
tale profits and the pillage
    and plunder of the
middle class – leaving in
    its wake shattered lives
and the perils of economic
    struggle to cast its dark
shadow on a barren land
    scape of confusion and
fear where the spoils of
    unfettered, unregu-
lated, unrestrained greed
    fade quietly into the
anonymity of wealth,
    power, and privilege.

III

THIS AMERICAN MOMENT

"The way to destroy the family is to create such deep poverty that parents, working two or three jobs to survive... lose touch with each other, and their children grow up as strangers."[14]
- Salome

The dismantling of America's middle class prosperity by the conservative *special interest* establishment in the quest for unlimited wealth betrayed "Main Street America" and

left the people of America
to exist and endure in
an impoverished *Subsist
ence Trickle-Down
Society.*

Lost is America's ability
to employ its people
with secure living-wage
jobs; lost to the people
of America is any realistic
expectation of afforda-
ble housing, food, trans-
portation, education,
and healthcare; while the
elderly of America in
the hundreds of
thousands, Americans
who've labored all their

lives, barely exist on
$800 or less a month. This
is the reality of the
American condition in
this American moment.

See for yourself, walk
with me for a moment
down freedom's road; let
us together get a
glimpse of how the
people of America see
the perpetual hardship
and tragedy of life in
this American moment.

There - in the distance, I
see two people talking;
Come - if we hurry - we

can listen in to what they're saying. Edging closer, we hear one confide to the other:

'Today I bear witness to the duplicity, inequity, and pretension of this American moment;

'Today I face the frustration, uncertainty, and despair of a people living "in quiet desperation;"[15]

'Today I endure the ordeal, misery, and

distress of a proud industrious people;'

'Today I struggle to survive the betrayal, corruption, and desolation of Dereg- ulation, Free Trade, and the Robber Barons of this American moment;

'Today I know this day is my every day for all my tomorrows.' [16]

I feel a profound sense of bewilderment and fore- boding. As I hesitate to

reflect on America's
special interest cunning
and political intrigue in
the mad dash to seize the
wealth of America -

I see my country drown-
ing in a wilderness of
greed and the debt of a
rich man's folly from
years of war waged on
borrowed money;
special interest tax code
accommodations;
special interest trillion-
dollar tax cuts; *special
interest* offshore tax
havens; *special interest*
tax holidays; *special*

interest trillion-dollar
taxpayer bailouts; *special
interest* government
welfare subsidies; *special
interest* speculation,
financial growth
gimmicks, loan shark
interest rates; the *special
interest* lobby politick,
and political campaign
financing.

I see my country suffering
under the oppressive
burden of *special interest*
crony capitalism,
robbed of its economic
security, impoverished
through Deregulation and

Free Trade politics, and
abandoned by a
    compromised political
machine reluctant to
    protect and defend the
security of the middle
    class and the stability of
the American family.

I sense all around me the
    overwhelming devasta-
tion, decay, and suffering
    of the human "collat-
eral damage" thrust aside
    in the dismantling of
America's economic prosperity.

I see the faces of the
   hungry and the
homeless; I feel the
   distress, the torment,
and the despair of the
   poor, the downtrodden,
and the oppressed of this
   American moment.

I hear from afar the
   distant thunder of ages
past trumpeting the sad
   lament of a patriot in a
similar time -

   *"I look with compas-
   sion upon the cruel
   tempest with which
   my country is threat-*

ened … (I) shed tears to see so many reduced to such a profound misery."[17]

IV

THE POORING OF AMERICA

"America's megabanks and policy makers are continuing a program... the ultimate result of which will be to virtually eliminate the middle class majority in America."[18]
-Richard Clark,
Why is America Suffering

Jobs! Jobs! Jobs! Where are the jobs? In this American world "turned upside down," over 50,000 of America's plants and factories closed before the turn of the century, another

60,000 plants have
    disappeared since 2000,
and some 90,000
    American factories are
presently pending closure.

By virtue of America's
    deindustrialized
economy through
    deregulation, free
trade, and changes in the
    tax code, China is the
manufacturing power-
    house of the world,
America's communities
    are bankrupt,
America's infrastructure
    is crumbling, and the
people of America are

struggling in a jobless *Subsistence Minimum-Wage Economy.*

The "pooring of America" is the story of *special interest* greed in the pursuit of cheap labor, big profits, and unlimited wealth; it is the saga of the "betrayal" of the American people by the conservative business and finance advocates of "laissez-faire" capitalism in the early nineteen seventies to reverse liberal public opinion, dominate the American political process, and deregulate American business and finance on the pretext govern- ment regulation and oversight was undermin- ing the American free enterprise system.

In the nineteen seventies and ensuing decades the American political scene degenerated into a divisive political drama of vulgar confrontation politics; America's world of business and finance was deregulated - freed from government

regulatory oversight; and
   the conservative *special
interest* political
   establishment achieved
the implementation of the
   deregulated free-trade
*Subsistence Minimum-
   Wage Economy*; the
dismantling of America's
   industrial prosperity;
the outsourcing of
   America's jobs,
production, and services;
   and finally, the
realization of America's
   jobless *Subsistence
Trickle-Down Society.*

The *Subsistence
    Minimum-Wage Economy*
and the *Subsistence
    Trickle-Down Society* are
the fulfillment of the
    conservative *special
interest* political agenda of
    unfettered, unrestrained,
    unlimited wealth at any cost
    laissez-faire capitalism,
and the *"every man for
    himself"* impoverished
middle class America.

And then behold came the
    "jewel in the crown" of
American deregulation
    politics. With the 1999
legislative "veto-proof"

repeal of the critical provisions of the Glass-Steagall Act Banking Act of 1933 engineered by key political figures of the conservative political establishment, the last of the great financial reforms of the Great Depression was no more. The repeal of government's ability to regulate and oversee America's financial institutions that had kept the "robber barons" at bay for over fifty years left the people of America open to financial corruption,

mortgage fraud,
   and financial collapse.

America's great financial
   disaster emerged in the
wake of a five billion dollar
   ten-year financial sector
campaign that led to the end
   of government regulatory
oversight of the financial
   services industry; the
repeal of Glass-Steagall;
   and the passage of the
Financial Services
   Modernization Act
of 1999, and Commodity
   Futures Modernization
Act of 2000 that made
   derivatives transactions

and credit default swaps
   exempt from government
regulation.

The conservative political
   deregulation of the
financial services industry
   achieved, there followed
the Fraudulent Energy
   Crisis and the Enron
Embezzlement Collapse that
   caused investors some 70
billion dollars; the rise of
   "too big to fail" megabanks; the onset of toxic
   unregulated financial
growth gimmicks; the
   Madoff Embezzlement
Scandal; 2007 Sub-Prime

Mortgage Crisis; 2007
Banking Crisis; 2008 Oil
Speculation Crisis; and
the 2008 Financial Collapse
that caused the national
debt to increase by some 11
trillion dollars; a carefully
orchestrated 14 trillion
dollar taxpayer bailout
delivered against the
expressed wishes of the
people; millions of jobs lost;
America's retirement
savings lost; eight million
American homes lost to
foreclosure; the Mortgage
Foreclosure Signing
Fraud Scandal; seven
trillion dollars of housing

wealth lost; the transfer of
    America's middle class
wealth to the one percent,
    and the realization of all
new wealth going to the one
    percent.

The "pooring of America"
    is the political and
economic reality of this
    American moment. Four
decades of political
    cunning, deceit, and
hypocrisy advancing the
    conservative *special
interest* agenda succeeded
    in bringing about the
deregulation of the rule of
    law in American business

and finance; trillion-dollar
   tax cuts and tax code
adjustments for the
   megarich and big
business; an American
   "trade deficit" of some 10
trillion dollars since 1976;
   tens of thousands of
America's businesses lost
   to the proliferation of
hostile takeovers and
   massive megamergers in
the creation of financial and
   corporate monopolies;
and the countless millions of
   American workers cast
aside as "just collateral
   damage." This is the cost
and sacrifice to the people of

America in the making of the *Subsistence Minimum-Wage Economy.*

Today's America is the political fulfillment of the conservative *special interest* economic agenda for the control of the people and wealth of America: today there are 18 million vacant homes in America; over four million Americans homeless; one in two Americans living in poverty; two of every three working Americans living on a minimum-wage income; 17

million households that
don't have enough food; 93
million unemployed
Americans struggling to
make it through another
day; 60 percent of personal
bankruptcies resulting
from medical bills; while
400 of the richest people
in America own more than
50 percent of America's
wealth, and one-tenth of one
percent of Americans
possess more wealth than
the bottom 90 percent.

In the absence of a return to
an America of political
and economic justice, the

elimination of what
remains of today's middle
class is all but assured
given the present reality of
the *Subsistence Trickle-
Down Society*; scarcity of
living-wage jobs; stagnant
1960s-level wages, and the
impoverishment of the
average American family.

History's alternative to
comprehensive political and
economic reform would
suggest the advent of a new
American epoch, a post-
modern feudal age of
imperial wealth, political
aristocracy, ruling elite,

class distinctions, and contract low-wage labor; a democracy of illusion, restricted civil liberties, limited individual education; conditional property ownership, mandated economic obligations; and a new era of singular responsibility in an austere American existence "of every man for himself" in *a conservative world without Social Security, Medicare, and Unemployment Insurance.*

Is this to be America's
    world of tomorrow? Just
consider *the* jobless
    Subsistence Minimum-
Wage Economy of this
    American moment as the
realization of an interim
    objective in the
conservative *special interest*
    blueprint in the creation
of the deregulated laissez-
    faire crony capitalist
"every man for himself" 21st
    Century America!

The question for this
    American Moment is
simply whether or not we
    the people of America are

willing to accept this new
   American 'trickle-down'
feudal world of tomorrow to
   be the legacy of our
children's future!

V

WHO DO WE SAY WE ARE

"These are times that try men's souls"... but then ... "We have it in our power to begin the world over again."
-Thomas Paine [19]

America – "We the
People" of this Ameri-
can moment, who do we
say we are?

America – Are we not a
people nurtured,
raised, and educated in
an America "of the
people, by the people, for

the people,"[20] an America
of "one nation under
God… with liberty and
justice for all"?[21]

America – Are we not a
people who've an-
swered the call of free-
dom for over two
hundred years, shedding
our blood on a
thousand battlefields?

America – Are we not the
children of yesterday's
heroes who vanquished
fascism, triumphed
over communism, and
labored to create the

great American economic
  miracle of full employ-
ment, living family wage,
  retirement pensions,
and affordable homes,
  education, and medical
care?

America – Are we not a
  people in this American
moment who bear wit-
  ness to the ordeal,
misery, and distress of
  unfettered runaway
capitalism, a people
  suffering in every
village, in every city, in
  every town; a people
struggling in a jobless

Subsistence Trickle-Down Society of massive income inequality; consumer household debt in the trillions of dollars; children residing with their parents into adulthood – jobless and saddled with a lifetime of student debt, hoping for a job at Walmart; and tens of millions of unemployed Americans hopeful each day for a few minimum-wage part-time hours of work?

America – Are we not a people whose national

legislature in this
  American moment is
dominated by a conser-
  vative political agenda
committed to obstruct,
  undermine, paralyze,
and demonize the
  executive branch; block
populace legislation and
  government funding
of social programs; dis-
  mantle Social Security,
Medicare, and Unem-
  ployment Insurance;
minimize *special interest*
  taxation; repudiate
man made climate
  change; champion
voter suppression; and

compel the American
people to assume the
national debt of a rich
man's folly not of the
people's making?

America – Are we not a
people whose great
democracy of Washing-
ton, Jefferson, and
Lincoln has been hijacked
from the people by a
political *special interest*
juggernaut funded by
"legalized" political
corruption in pursuit of
power and wealth at any
cost; the deregulation of
the rule of law in

business and finance;
the dissolution of
America's ability to
employ its people, and the
pooring of America's
middle class America?

America - Are we not a
people who bear witness
to the tragedy of this
American moment
betrayed, sacrificed, and
abandoned – a people
betrayed by the people's
elected representatives
to the power and money
of *special interests*; a
people *sacrificed* in the
name of wealth and

profit for the sole benefit
of *special interests*; a
people *abandoned* jobless
and impoverished in a
*Subsistence Trickle-Down
Society* created by
special interests for *special
interests*?

America – Are we not a
people born of our
fathers' sacrifice for an
America of Freedom,
Equality, and Justice, a
people responsible in
each generation to *protect,
defend, and preserve the
"Blessings of Liberty"* –
those democratic *con-*

stitutional guarantees
    that ensure the sover-
eignty and dominion of
    the people?

America – Are we not a
    people whose time has
come to face the political
    reality of this American
moment "as a people"
    committed to
participate in the
    democratic process on
Election Day with an
    understanding of the
issues that will determine
    the availability of
sufficient productive full-
    time jobs, a living

family wage; and provide
for the security and
stability of the American
family?

American – Are we not a
people whose time has
come to ask ourselves who
we are; what we want
"as a people" in this
American Moment;
what we hope to leave our
children and future
generations?

America - Are we not a
*people conceived in
Liberty with "the right, the
power, the duty"* [22] *... "to*

*begin the world over
   again?"*[23]Surely our
tomorrows need not be the
   "trickle-down" here and
now of this American
   moment.

America – Are we not a
   people whose time has
come to *confront* the
   corruption of "Corpor-
ate Personhood, "Citizens
   United," and "taxation
without representation;"
   demand an end to the
pillage and plunder of
   institutional greed;
insist on the restoration of
   the "rule of law" in

business, finance, and the
    courts, and *reclaim* for
all America Liberty's
    promise of Freedom,
Equality, and Justice?

America – look – listen –
    see, *there rises* across
the American heartland a
    release of the American
spirit, a *great awakening*
    of a people acutely
aware of the frustration,
    uncertainty, and despair
of this American moment;
    a people pledged to a
new commitment to
    return representative
government to the will of

the people; a *new resolve* to ensure every American has access to a full-time living wage job, and every individual and business pay their fair share; a *new beginning* for a struggling people and the future of America – ever mindful – *how we live as a people tomorrow will be what we are willing to accept "as a people" in this American moment.*

America – "We the People" of these United States of America, who do we say we are?

VI

WE THE PEOPLE

"We the People" of
   America, we are the life-
blood of freedom and
   democracy in America;
the defender of America's
   promise of "Life,
Liberty and the Pursuit
   of Happiness;"[24] the
Beacon of Liberty to the
   world's oppressed.

"We the People" of
   America, we are a
people "Conceived in Lib-
erty"[25] - democracy's

covenant of freedom and justice for all; a people suffering from decades of corruption for the enrichment of a few; a people who today see a "clear and present danger"[26] to the inviolability of the United States Constitution and the "Blessings of Liberty;"[27] a people with *the right, the power, the duty*[28] to make right the income inequality, the suffering, and the injustices of the *Jobless Subsistence Minimum-Wage Society* of this American moment.

"We the People" of America, we are a people nurtured from birth to honor, protect, and defend Liberty's promise of Freedom, Equality and Justice; a people triumphant across the generations from Lexington and Concord to the Sea of Tranquility; a people who in this American moment struggle to contain poverty, labor to keep America strong, and protect America in these perilous times.

"We the People" of this
   American moment, let
all bear witness to who we
   are:

WE THE PEOPLE
WE ARE AMERICA!

A people of hope "In God
   We Trust"[29] confident
the light of a new dawn
   beckons to brighten our
tomorrow.

A COUNTRY DIVIDED
A Citizen's Plea for An America
of Political and Economic Justice

"Let us not seek to fix the blame for the past. Let us accept our own responsibility for the future."[30] -
John F. Kennedy

When I look around me, open up the newspaper, turn on the evening news, I see 'a country divided.' I see an America unrecognizable from the days of my youth not so long ago. I see a state of being in America where less than 1% of America's population own more wealth than the bottom 90% of the people of America; where 400 individuals possess as much wealth as the bottom 58% of America - that would be the 180 million Americans who live poor in the *Subsistence Trickle-Down Society* of this American moment.

In my shock, frustration, and disbelief, I cannot help but ask, "How can this be? How can such inequality and injustice be present in an America dedicated to the democratic principles of Freedom, Equality, and Justice?"

Surely we are a people who from infancy understand we are a people conceived in Liberty; a people whose Constitution guarantees the inalienable rights of the individual, and a political mandate for the people's elected representative government "to protect the general welfare" of the people. To any reasonable person I would think this Constitutional affirmation "to protect the general welfare" enacted by the Founding Fathers, is a political covenant that ensures every person the right to pursue happiness, and obligates the people's government to exercise its duty and responsibility to protect the welfare and well-being of its citizens, that is – it is the responsibility of government to assure the nation has sufficient living-wage jobs to adequately employ its people; maintains a viable national infrastructure; provides available affordable national healthcare; offers affordable educational opportunity; and, most importantly, enforces the exercise of legal oversight protection for the people from predatory interests.

It is by virtue of who we are as a free democratic people at a political crossroads of failed politics that we are a people fascinated, if not captivated, with the politics of a non-establishment social progressive who dares speak the truth, and rally the American people against the poverty, misery, and despair of the repressive jobless *Subsistence Tricke-Down Society* of this America moment and the visible ever present demise of the middle class.

We must recognize today's political crisis as the culmination of forty years of assault on the Constitution, long-established laws safeguarding the public interest, and the welfare of the people of America. From the appearance of the "Powell Memorandum" in 1971 and the advent of the "Business Roundtable"

in 1972, the conservative business and finance advocates of laissez-faire crony capitalism over a
period of three decades success-
fully overpowered the American
political system with money and
lobbyists, and through the deregulation of business and finance,
free trade policies, and changes in
the tax code dismantled America's
industrial might, and brought
about the *Subsistence Minimum-
Wage Economy* of today's forgotten
impoverished America.

And so when we consider the political crisis of this American
moment, the despair and hope-
-lessness of decades living under
the economic repression of the
Subsistence Trickle-Down Society,
and the anger, fear, and resent-

ment of political crony capitalism, we find we are people who look to a non-establishment social progressive as we ask ourselves who we are, where we are going, and what is to be the America of our children's tomorrow.

When the same old political rhetoric that promises to address the plight of the American condition comes up short, it should not come as a surprise to anyone we are a people asking the very simple question - why? *"Why, you our elected representatives, why have of you abandoned us? Why, you in whom we have placed our trust, why have you forsaken your people?"*

Of course the straight answer is the unmitigated shameless hypocrisy of the corruption of political power, an across the board absence of law and regulation in business and finance, unregulated campaign financing, and universal political cronyism. In the end it is this sad reality of America's crony capitalism and the vulgar confrontation politics of this America moment that we are a people crying out for a national leader with a vision 'to believe in' that promises to remedy the crisis in leadership dominated by special interests and the tragedy of the American condition for most of the people of America.

I was somewhat surprised recently to hear the news media report the onset of talk, or might I say, unease, within the conservative establishment on the need to preserve the "core principles" and "ideological purity" of American conservatism. Now as I ponder the *record of betrayal of American conservatism* over the last forty years, I see clearly the reality of those common *"core principles"* of American conservatism, common core principles that fostered the ideological predatory initiatives that handed America over to the corruption of unfettered, unregulated, unrestrained laissez-faire crony capitalism; common *"core principles"* that made possible the money and lobbyists that forged an America subjected to decades of stagnation, decay, poverty and suffering.

I have for decades witnessed first-hand the stampede of conservative *"core values"* across America – *"core values"* that have transformed the America political scene into vulgar confrontation politics; *"core values"* that made possible the *Subsistence Trickle-Down Society*; *"core values"* that sold the American people false promises of "tax cuts" to fuel the economy and "free trade" agreements to create higher paying jobs for America.

But the conservative assault of *false promises* thrust upon the people of America realized only misery, uncertainty, and despair, political initiatives that have overwhelmed the American people with income inequality; outsourced jobs; wage stagnation; wealthy tax cuts contributing trillions of dollars to the national debt; corporate tax loopholes; corporate welfare subsidies; 'for profit' healthcare no one can afford; "for profit" prisons requiring 90 percent occupancy; repeal and defunding of social programs protecting the "general welfare"; restriction of vital civil liberties; limitations on voting rights; suppression of worker's rights; and passage of legislation contrary to the wishes of the American people that enacted the *fourteen trillion dollar socialist tax-payer bailout* of America's failed laissez-faire roulette financial capitalism.

This is today's American fairy- tale world of conservative crony capitalist greed of quick profits over people at any cost engendered and fostered through the dismissal of the rule of law, unequal trade, and the privatization of government assets and public services.

We need only look at any community in America and there lies the fruits of the conservative *Trickle-Down Economic Agenda* – communities impoverished and bankrupt; infrastructure crumbling; austere school budgets; community industrial tax base gone; and massive unemployment due to the dismantled industrial America driven by greed, power, and wealth in the chase for cheap labor and fairy-tale profits. And yet, there persists today among the conservative political establishment an insistence on national fiscal austerity at the expense of the American people, an austerity obligating the people

of America to pay for a multi-tril-
lion dollar national debt 'of a rich
man's folly not of the people's making' while, at the same time, openly
promoting more tax cuts for the
rich that will substantially enlarge
the national debt in the trillions of
dollars.

In this American moment 'a country divided' we are – a people struggling day-to-day to survive a predatory *Subsistence Trickle-Down
Society* of 93 million unemployed
working age Americans; two out of
three working Americans earning
a minimum-wage that cannot support the basic necessities of life; and
one in two Americans living poor -
coexisting with another America of
immense wealth concentrated in
the hands of a few, an America of

wealth and privilege legislated by the special interest crony politics of trickle-down economics, deregulation, tax code adjustments, periodic tax cuts, and a *conservative promise kept of no new taxes for the America of wealth, power, and privilege.*

The time has come to ask, *"How much is enough?"* Today, "We the People" of America DECLARE to you our elected representatives: *"This land we call home is our America too. The time has come for political and economic justice. The time has come to open the road to prosperity to all Americans. The time has come for everybody to pay their share.*

The time has come to say *"NO MORE": 'no more'* deregulation; *'no more'* wealthy tax cuts; *'no more'* special interest welfare subsidies, tax loopholes, and off-shore tax havens; *'no more'* unequal trade agreements, hostile takeovers, megamergers, and outsourcing of American jobs; 'no *more'* financial manipulation and commodities speculation, user fee piracy, loan shark interest rates, and unregulated financial growth gimmicks"

Today "We the People" of America SAY TO YOU who are want to represent the people's interests: *"The time is now that we come together to rebuild an America for all Americans: return* the rule of law to business, finance, the courts, and the democratic electoral process; *provide* the people of America with productive living wage jobs, affordable universal healthcare and higher education; and *ensure* the financial viability of Social Security and Medicare through progressive funding legislation that assures all Americans the right to retire and live out their senior years in dignity and respect.

Today we are a people who REPRUDIATE, DISAVOW AND CONDEMN the ravages and devastation of unfettered unregulated laissez-faire capitalism, an American evil brought about through the deception and deceit of a cunning political crony establishment that knowingly and willingly conspired to betray and forever condemn the people of America to the institutionalized

poverty and misery of the "robber baron" *Subsistence Minimum-
Wage Economy* of cheap labor and
windfall profits.

"We the People" of America in this
time of political decision DEMAND
that you our elected representatives
*REDRESS the injustices, iniquity,
and corruption of the laissez-faire
crony political capitalism of this
American moment that plagues
the American body politic of a free
democratic people, and fosters the
Subsistence Trickle-Down Society
of this American moment.*

Now my journey here I see drawing
to a close, and I find my troubled
thoughts once again adrift along
freedom's road pondering Liberty's promise of Freedom, Equal-

ity, and Justice, that age old covenant of blood and sacrifice with an America that forever cherishes and defends the freedom, well-being, and happiness of every citizen.

Through the dismal fog of silent desperation, distain, and disquiet of a sacrificed abandoned people, I see a hurting America cry out for justice. I see a proud patriotic people engulfed in the economic quagmire of failed politics. I see the everyday anguish, despair, and hopelessness of a people suffering. I see evident far and near the portent of America's pain.

As I pause to face the blowing tempest knock at freedom's door, I see a people of hope longing to overcome the injustices of this Ameri-

can moment. I see before me a renewal of the American Spirit and
the makings of a coming new age
of Freedom, Equality, and Justice.

But the advent of the coming new
age of democratic freedoms is now.
America's 21st Century will be
what "We the People" of America
decide in this American moment,
for we are still a democratic people who have the political right and
the power to do nothing or take a
stand to right the political and economic injustices of the *Subsistence
Trickle-Down Society.*

In this difficult and distressing time
of American political crony capitalism, vulgar confrontation politics,
and conservative ideological ob-
structionism, the political and eco-

nomic injustices of this American moment give sufficient cause for alarm to suggest we seriously reflect "as a people" on history's most sober and somber cautionary reminder: that only a politically free sovereign people in control of its own political destiny can and will provide for the future freedom and prosperity of generations to come.

The extent "We the People" of America are willing to *"accept our own responsibility"*[31] to exercise *"the right, the power, and the duty to protect (our) own welfare"*[32] in this hour of political decision will be of paramount significance in the making of America's democratic world of tomorrow.

"We the People" of America, may we come together "as a people" determined to redeem our democratic heritage of Freedom, Equality, and Justice, and restore this great nation "of the people, by the people, for the people"[33] to the sovereignty and dominion of the governed of this American moment.

"We the People," let us today give thanks for America's democratic legacy of Washington, Jefferson, and Lincoln, and together proudly proclaim:

GOD BLESS AMERICA!

What you see ... is a system of govern-ment that seems incapable of action. You see a Congress twisted and pulled in every direction by hundreds of well-financed and powerful *special in-terests* ... What can we do? ... We must face the truth, and then we can change our course ..." [34]

President Jimmy Carter,
Crisis of Confidence

COMMENTARY

"Courage is what preserves
our liberty, safety, life, and
our homes and parents, our
country and children."
                    -Plautus

On Democracy

On Liberty

On Politics

On Poverty

On Special Interests

ON DEMOCRACY

"If liberty and equality are to be found in democracy, they will be but attained when all persons alike share in government to the utmost."[35]

-**Aristotle**

"Let us never forget that government is ourselves ... The ultimate rulers are not a President and senators and congressmen and government officials, but the voters of this country."[36]

-**Franklin D. Roosevelt**

"We must make our choice. We may have democracy, or we may have wealth concentrated in the hands of a few, but we can't have both."

-**Louis D. Brandeis**

ON LIBERTY

"Free people, remember ... we may acquire liberty, but it is never recovered if it is lost."[37]
-Jean-Jacques Rousseau

"Either democracy must be renewed, with politics brought back to life, or wealth is likely to cement a new or less democratic regime – plutocracy by some other name."[38]
-Kevin Phillips

"When the people fear the government there is tyranny, when the government fears the people there is liberty."
-John Basil Barnhill

ON POLITICS

"The most perfect political community is one in which the middle class is in control, and outnumbers both of the other classes."[39]

-Aristotle

"The political machine triumphs because it is a united minority against a divided majority."[40]

-Will Durant

"Let us wage a moral and political war against the billionaires and corporate leaders ... whose policies and greed are dismantling the middle class of America."

-Bernie Sanders

ON POVERTY

"Where injustice is denied, where poverty is enforced, where ignorance prevails, and where any one class is made to feel that society is an organized conspiracy to oppress, rob and degrade them, neither persons nor property will be safe."[41]
-Frederick Douglass

"In a country well governed, poverty is something to be ashamed of. In a country badly governed, wealth is something to be ashamed of."[42]
-Confucius

"Poverty is the absence of all human rights. The frustrations, hostility, and anger generated by object poverty cannot sustain peace in any society."[43]
-Yunus

ON SPECIAL INTERESTS

"The government, which was designed for the people, has gotten into the hands of ... special interests. An invisible empire has been set up above the forms of democracy."
-Jimmy Carter

"Behind the ostensible government sits enthroned an invisible government owing no allegiance and acknowledging no responsibility to the people."
-Theodore Roosevelt

"These are very powerful and wealthy special interests who want to privatize or dismember virtually every function that government now performs, whether it is Social Security, Medicare, public education or the Postal Service."
-Bernie Sanders

APPENDIX

"Policy is no longer being written by politicians accountable to the American public. Instead, policies concerning the defense budget, deregulation, health care ... are now largely written by lobbyists who represent mega-corporations."
                                    - Henry Giroux [44]

BILL OF RIGHTS OF THE UNITED STATES CONSTITUTION

DECLARATION OF INDEPENDENCE

BILL OF RIGHTS
OF THE
UNITED STATES CONSTITUTION

I
Freedom of Speech, Press, Religion and Petition

Congress shall make no law respecting an establishment of religion, or prohibiting the free exercise thereof; or abridging the freedom of speech, or of the press; or the right of the people peaceably to assemble, and to petition the Government for a redress of grievances.

II
Right to keep and bear arms

A well-regulated militia, being necessary to the security of a free State, the right of the people to keep and bear arms, shall not be infringed.

III
Conditions for quarters of soldiers

No soldier shall, in time of peace be quartered in any house, without the consent of the owner, nor in time of war, but in a manner to be prescribed by law.

IV
Right of search and seizure regulated

The right of the people to be secure in their persons, houses, papers, and effects, against unreasonable searches and seizures, shall not be violated, and no warrants shall issue, but upon probable cause, supported by oath or affirmation, and particularly describing the place to be searched, and the persons or things to be seized.

V
Provisions concerning prosecution

No person shall be held to answer for a capital, or otherwise infamous crime, unless on a presentment or indictment of a Grand Jury, except in cases arising in the land or naval forces, or in the militia, when in actual service in time of war or public danger; nor shall any person be subject for the same offense to be twice put in jeopardy of life or limb; nor shall be compelled in any criminal case to be a witness against himself, nor be deprived of life, liberty, or property, without due process of law; nor shall private property be taken for public use without just compensation.

VI
Right to a speedy trial, witnesses, etc.

In all criminal prosecutions, the accused shall enjoy the right to a speedy and public trial, by an impartial jury of the State and district wherein the crime shall have been committed, which district shall have been previously ascertained by law, and to be informed of the nature and cause of the accusation; to be confronted with the witnesses against him; to have compulsory process for obtaining witnesses in his favor, and to have the assistance of counsel for his defense.

VII
Right to a trial by jury

In suits at common law, where the value in controversy shall exceed twenty dollars, the right of trial by jury shall be preserved, and no fact tried by a jury shall be otherwise reexamined in any court of the United States, than according to the rules of the common law.

VIII
Excessive bail, cruel punishment

Excessive bail shall not be required, nor excessive fines imposed, nor cruel and unusual punishments inflicted.

IX
Rule of construction of Constitution

The enumeration in the Constitution, of certain rights, shall not be construed to deny or disparage others retained by the people.

X
Rights of the States under Constitution

The powers not delegated to the United States by the Constitution, nor prohibited by it to the States, are reserved to the States respectively, or to the people.

U.S. National Archives and Records
Administration
(www.archives.gov)

The Declaration of Independence
(A Transcription)

IN CONGRESS, July 4, 1776.

The unanimous Declaration of the thirteen united States of America,

When in the Course of human events, it becomes necessary for one people to dissolve the political bands which have connected them with another, and to assume among the powers of the earth, the separate and equal station to which the Laws of Nature and of Nature's God entitle them, a decent respect to the opinions of mankind requires that they should declare the causes which impel them to the separation.

We hold these truths to be self-evident, that all men are created equal, that they are endowed by their Creator with certain unalienable Rights, that among these are Life, Liberty and the pursuit of Happiness.--That to secure these rights, Governments are instituted among Men, deriving their just powers from the consent of the governed, --That whenever any Form of Government becomes destructive of these ends, it is the Right of the People to alter or to abolish it, and to institute new Government, laying its foundation on such principles and organizing its powers in such form, as to them shall seem most likely to affect their Safety and Happiness. Prudence, indeed, will dictate that Governments long established should not be changed for light and transient causes; and accordingly all experience hath shewn, that mankind are more disposed to suffer, while evils are sufferable, than to right themselves by abolishing the forms to which they are accustomed. But when a long train of abuses and usurpations, pursuing invariably the same Object evinces a design to reduce them under absolute Despotism, it is their right, it is their duty, to throw off such Government, and to provide new Guards for their future security.--Such has been the patient sufferance of these Colonies; and such is now the necessity which constrains them to alter their former Systems of Government. The history of the present King of Great Britain is a history of repeated injuries and usurpations, all having in direct object the establishment of an absolute Tyranny over these States. To prove this, let Facts be submitted to a candid world.

He has refused his Assent to Laws, the most wholesome and necessary for the public good.

He has forbidden his Governors to pass Laws of immediate and pressing importance, unless suspended in their operation till his Assent should be obtained; and when so suspended, he has utterly neglected to attend to them.

He has refused to pass other Laws for the accommodation of large districts of people, unless those people would relinquish the right of Representation in the Legislature, a right inestimable to them and formidable to tyrants only.

He has called together legislative bodies at places unusual, uncomfortable, and distant from the depository of their public Records, for the sole purpose of fatiguing them into compliance with his measures.

He has dissolved Representative Houses repeatedly, for opposing with manly firmness his invasions on the rights of the people.

He has refused for a long time, after such dissolutions, to cause others to be elected; whereby the Legislative powers, incapable of Annihilation, have returned to the People at large for their exercise; the State remaining in the meantime exposed to all the dangers of invasion from without, and convulsions within.

He has endeavoured to prevent the population of these States; for that purpose obstructing the Laws for Naturalization of Foreigners; refusing to pass others to encourage their migrations hither, and raising the conditions of new Appropriations of Lands.

He has obstructed the Administration of Justice, by refusing his Assent to Laws for establishing Judiciary powers.

He has made Judges dependent on his Will alone, for the tenure of their offices, and the amount and payment of their salaries.

He has erected a multitude of New Offices, and sent hither swarms of

Officers to harass our people, and eat out their substance.

He has kept among us, in times of peace, Standing Armies without the Consent of our legislatures.

He has affected to render the Military independent of and superior to the Civil power.

He has combined with others to subject us to a jurisdiction foreign to our constitution, and unacknowledged by our laws; giving his Assent to their Acts of pretended Legislation:

For Quartering large bodies of armed troops among us:

For protecting them, by a mock Trial, from punishment for any Murders which they should commit on the Inhabitants of these States:

For cutting off our Trade with all parts of the world:

For imposing Taxes on us without our Consent:

For depriving us in many cases, of the benefits of Trial by Jury:

For transporting us beyond Seas to be tried for pretended offences:

For abolishing the free System of English Laws in a neighbouring Province, establishing therein an Arbitrary government, and enlarging its Boundaries so as to render it at once an example and fit instrument for introducing the same absolute rule into these Colonies:

For taking away our Charters, abolishing our most valuable Laws, and altering fundamentally the Forms of our Governments:

For suspending our own Legislatures, and declaring themselves invested with power to legislate for us in all cases whatsoever.

He has abdicated Government here, by declaring us out of his Protection and waging War against us.

He has plundered our seas, ravaged our Coasts, burnt our towns, and destroyed the lives of our people.

He is at this time transporting large Armies of foreign Mercenaries to compleat the works of death, desolation and tyranny, already begun with circumstances of Cruelty & perfidy scarcely paralleled in the most barbarous ages, and totally unworthy the Head of a civilized nation.

He has constrained our fellow Citizens taken Captive on the high Seas to bear Arms against their Country, to become the executioners of their friends and Brethren, or to fall themselves by their Hands.

He has excited domestic insurrections amongst us, and has endeavoured to bring on the inhabitants of our frontiers, the merciless Indian Savages, whose known rule of warfare, is an undistinguished destruction of all ages, sexes and conditions.

In every stage of these Oppressions We have Petitioned for Redress in the most humble terms: Our repeated Petitions have been answered only by repeated injury. A Prince whose character is thus marked by every act which may define a Tyrant, is unfit to be the ruler of a free people.

Nor have We been wanting in attentions to our British brethren. We have warned them from time to time of attempts by their legislature to extend an unwarrantable jurisdiction over us. We have reminded them of the circumstances of our emigration and settlement here. We have appealed to their native justice and magnanimity, and we have conjured them by the ties of our common kindred to disavow these usurpations, which, would inevitably interrupt our connections and correspondence. They too have been deaf to the voice of justice and of consanguinity. We must, therefore, acquiesce in the necessity, which denounces our Separation, and hold them, as we hold the rest of mankind, Enemies in War, in Peace Friends.

We, therefore, the Representatives of the united States of America, in General Congress, Assembled, appealing to the Supreme Judge of the world for the rectitude of our intentions, do, in the Name, and by Authority of the good

People of these Colonies, solemnly publish and declare, That these United Colonies are, and of Right ought to be Free and Independent States; that they are Absolved from all Allegiance to the British Crown, and that all political connection between them and the State of Great Britain, is and ought to be totally dissolved; and that as Free and Independent States, they have full Power to levy War, conclude Peace, contract Alliances, establish Commerce, and to do all other Acts and Things which Independent States may of right do. And for the support of this Declaration, with a firm reliance on the protection of divine Providence, we mutually pledge to each other our Lives, our Fortunes and our sacred Honor.

(56 signatures appear on the Declaration)

Page URL: http://www.archives.gov/exhibits/charters/declaration_transcript.html
U.S. National Archives & Records Admin.
8601 Adelphi Road, College Park, MD, 20740-6001, •
1-86-NARA-NARA • 1-866-272-6272

SUGGESTED READING

"Freedom is the right to tell people
what they do not want to hear." [45]
- **George Orwell**

Austin, Michael, *That's Not What They Meant!*
(Amherst, NY: Prometheus Books, 1992)

Bartlett, Donald L., and James B. Steele, *The
Betrayal of the American Dream* (NY: Public
Affairs, 2012)

Batra, Ravi, *The Pooring of America: Competi-
tion and the Myth of Free Trade* (NY: Collier
Books, 1993)

Crier, Catherine, *Patriot Acts* (NY: Threshold
Editiors, 2011)

Greider, William L., *Who Will Tell The People:
The Betrayal of American Democracy* (NY:
Simon and Schuster, 1992)

Hartmann, Thom, *The Crash of 2016:* The Plot to
Destroy America *(NY: Twelve, 2014)*

Klinknecht, William, *The Man Sold the World :
Ronald Reagan and the Betrayal of Main Street
America.* (NY: Nation Books, 2009)

Lefebvre, Georges, *The Coming of the French Revolution* (Princeton University Press, 1973)

Lessig, Lawrence, *Republic, Lost* (NY Hachette Book Group, 2011)

Lofgren, Mike, *The Party Is Over* (NY: Penguin Group, 2012)

Moyers, Bill *Moyers On Democracy* (NY: Anchor Books, 2007)

Murry, Charles, *Coming Apart* (NY: Crown Forum, 2012)

Phillips, Kevin *Wealth and Democracy: The Political History of the Rich* (NY: Broadway Books, 2003)

Reich, Robert B., *Beyond Outrage* (NY: Vintage Books, 2012)

Robison, James and Jay W. Richards, *Invisible: Restoring Faith, Family, and Freedom Before It's Too Late.* (NY: Faith Words, 2012)

Smith, Hedrick, *Who Stole the American Dream* (NY: Random House, 2012)

Woodward, Bob, *The Price of Politics* (NY: Simon & Schuster, 2012)

NOTES

"From 1998 through 2008, the finance
sector spent over $5 billion in lobbying
and campaign donations to deregulate
Wall Street."[46]
– Bernie Sanders

[1] "Something shattering ..." Donella Meadows,
Donella Meadows Archives, "Who will Tell the People
(http://www.donellameadows.org/archives/
who-will-tell-people)

[2] "Who Will Tell the People" William Greider, *Who Will
Tell the People : The Betrayal of American Democracy*
(NY: Simon and Schuster, 1992)

[3] "Money's conquest ..." Allison Stanger
*One Nation Under Contract: Six Questions for Allison
Stanger* (http://harpers.org/blog/2011/04/ one-nation-
under-contract)

[4] "Democracy arises ...." Aristotle
(http://www.brainyquote.com)

[5] "There's no nation ..." Daniel Webster
(http://goodreads.com/quotes/125747)

[6] "The business..." Donald L. Bartlett and James B. Steele,
The Betrayal of the American Dream (NY: Public Affairs,
2012)

[7] "of the people" *Gettysburg Address*, from Wikipedia, the
free encyclopedia (http://en.wikipedia.org)

[8] "liberty and justice ..." *Pledge of Allegiance*, from Wikipedia, the free encyclopedia (http://en.wikipedia.org)

[9] "We the People" *United States Constitution*, from Wikipedia," the free encyclopedia (http://en.wikipedia.org)

[10] "The right ..." "Theodore Roosevelt believed in pure democracy" from "Progressingamerica" (http://progressingamerica.blogspot.com)

[11] "The Promise of..." Charles R. Rangel (http://www.brainyquote.com)

[12] "one Nation ..." Op. cit. *Pledge of Allegiance*

[13] "Life, Liberty and ..." Thomas Jefferson *United States Declaration of Independence*, from Wikipedia, the free encyclopedia" (http://en.wikipedia.org)

[14] "The ... way to destroy ..." Salome (http://www.disgus.com/embed/com)

[15] "quiet desperation" Henry David Thoreau (http://www.brainyquote.com)

[16] "All My Tomorrows" M. G. Montpelier

[17] "I look with ..." Georges Lefebvre, *The Coming of the French Revolution* (Princeton University Press, 1947 & 1973)

[18] "America's Megabank's ..." Richard Clark, *Why is America Suffering ...* (http://www.opednews.com)

[19] "These are times … we have it in our power …" Thomas Paine (http://www.brainyquote.com).

[20] "of the people" *Gettysburg Address*, from Wikipedia, the free encyclopedia (http://en.wikipedia.org).

[21] "one Nation …" Ibid.

[22] "the regret …" Op. cit. Theodore Roosevelt.

[23] "to begin the …" Op. cit. Thomas Paine.

[24] "Life, Liberty and …" Thomas Jefferson
United States Declaration of Independence, from Wikipedia, the free encyclopedia" (http://en.wikipedia.org)

[25] "Conceived in Liberty" Op. cit. *Gettysburg Address;* Book by Murray Rothbard (Auburn, AL: Mises Institute, 2011) – Rothbard see the American Revolution as "a time libertarian radicalism." from Wikipedia, the free encyclopedia" (http://en.wikipedia.org)

[26] "Clear and present danger" "Clear and present danger was a doctrine adopted by the Supreme Court of the United States to determine under what circumstances limits can be placed on First Amendment freedoms of speech, press, or assembly."

[27] "Blessings …" Op. cit. *United States Constitution.*

[28] "the right, the power …" Op. cit. Theodore Roosevelt.

[29] "In God We Trust" Official motto of the United States" from Wikipedia, the free encyclopedia (http://en.wikipedia.org)

[30] "Let us not seek….." John F. Kennedy (http://www.brainyquote.com)

[31] "accept our….." John F. Kennedy (http://www.brainyquote.com)

[32] "the right …" Op. cit. Theodore Roosevelt (http://progressingamerica.blogspot.com)

[33] "of the people" *Gettysburg Address*, from Wikipedia, the free encyclopedia (http://en.wikipedia.org).

[34] "As I began to speak …" President Jimmy Carter from "Crisis of Confidence" speech, (http://www.pbs.org/wgbh/americanexperience/features/primary-resources/carter-crisis/)

[35] "If Liberty and …" Aristotle (http://www.brainyquote.com)

[36] "Let us never …" Franklin D. Roosevelt (http://www.brainyquote.com)

[37] "Free people …" Jean-Jacques Rousseau (http://www.brainyquote.com)

[38] "Either democracy must …" Kevin Phillips – noteworthy Quotes) http://www.adnola.org)

[39] "The most perfect …" Aristotle (http://www.brainyquote.com)

[40] "The political machine …" Will Durant (http://www.brainyquote.com)

[41] "Where injustice is ..." Frederick Douglas (http://www.brainyquote.com)

[42] "In a country..." Confucius (http://www.brainyquote.com)

[43] "Poverty is the ..." Yunus (http://www.brainyquote.com)

[44] "Policy is no longer ..." Henry Giroux (http://www.brainyquote.com).

[45] "Freedom is the ..." George Orwell (http://www.brainyquote.com).

[46] "From 1998 to ..." Bernie Sanders (http://www.brainyquote.com).

www.ingramcontent.com/pod-product-compliance
Lightning Source LLC
Chambersburg PA
CBHW051542170526
45165CB00002B/844